SOCIAL MEDIA STRATEGY FINANCIAL ADVISERS, I MANAGERS AND FINANCIAL PLANNERS

SOCIAL MEDIA STRATEGY PLANNER FOR FINANCIAL ADVISERS, IFAs, WEALTH MANAGERS AND FINANCIAL PLANNERS

Including a Value Based Social Media Strategy for Financial Advisers

By Philip Calvert

Copyright © 2019 Philip Calvert. All Rights Reserved.

This book or any portion thereof may not be reproduced or used in any manner whatsoever without the express written permission of the publisher except for the use of brief quotations in a book review or scholarly journal.

Cover photo by William Iven

ISBN: 978-1-703-98484-2

Contents

Part 1: Value Based Social Media Strategy for Financial Advisers

Part 2: Social Media Strategy Planner

Additional Resources for Financial Advisers

About the Author

Disclaimer and Terms of Use

Part 1:

Value Based Social Media Strategy for Financial Advisers

Thank you for your interest in this guide – I hope you'll find it useful.

There are many different ways that Financial Advisers can use Social Media in their businesses – in fact we've identified thirty-eight separate outcomes that advisers could expect to see from strategic use of Social tools such as Facebook, LinkedIn, Twitter, YouTube et al.

In this guide, we'll overview just one possible Social Media strategy that a financial advice firm might create.

I'm calling it a **Value Based Social Media Strategy**, and it's a process which is designed to build relationships with prospects who find you online and eventually convert some of them into purchasers of your highest value service.

For some Financial Advisers this might be a full financial planning process and for others it might be an ongoing coaching programme. It can also be something else, and ultimately it will depend on what you offer within your own financial advice business.

Although the Internet has become the de facto method for consumers to find, review, assess, refer and initially engage with Financial Advisers, it's no guarantee that a visit to your website will result in someone wanting to become a client. In fact, our research amongst Financial Advisers showed that as many as 73% of visitors to an IFA's website left without looking at another page.

This is known as the 'bounce rate' and a great many Financial Adviser's sites (in the UK) are shocked to discover that their rate is around 63 per cent. And that's not good at all.

The key issue is not necessarily one of driving traffic to a website, but more of converting the traffic into a good quality lead. But that said, most Financial Advisers are still not using Social Media very well at all to drive traffic to their websites in the first place, and that's largely because they don't have a Social Media strategy.

So what follows is a specimen plan designed to

    a) drive traffic to your website, and
    b) convert it into clients.

Sounds good? Then read on.

Please note that when I use the word 'IFA' in this text, I'm using it as a broad and generic term for any Financial Advice professional, Financial Planner, RIA, Wealth Manager or Financial Life Planner wherever you are in the world. Here in the UK where I'm based, it's a term that has been adopted widely over many years, even if it doesn't completely accurately reflect your status as an adviser. I hope you can bear with me – thank you!

You'll need to read this guide in conjunction with the chalkboard graphic. There's a copy below but if you would like us to email you a larger full colour copy, please get in touch at philip@philipcalvert.com

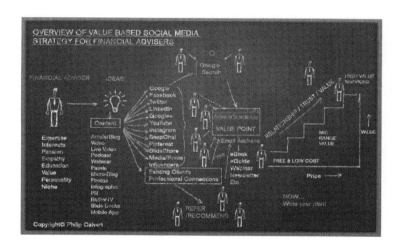

Column 1: You, the Adviser

If you look at the left-hand side of the chalkboard graphic (column 1), you'll find our adviser. He or she has a variety of attributes and characteristics which will attract people to them. These include amongst other things:

- *Expertise* gained over several years working with clients within the financial advice profession

- *Interests* outside work which will resonate with potential clients

- *Passion* for their work and the outcomes they help clients to achieve in their lives

- *Empathy* and understanding of clients' needs

- *Education* and credibility gained through examination and ongoing professional development

- *Value* to give to clients – perhaps through customer service or a unique client proposition

- *Personality* and humour. Remember, people buy people!

- *Niche expertise* which is of great value to certain groups of people

Combine these attributes and characteristics together and every Financial Adviser has something incredibly unique to offer which goes way beyond simply offering financial advice.

Financial Advice is not just given face to face

Financial advice or planning always used to be something which was only done between 'consenting adults' either in your office or their home - but thanks to the Internet, financial expertise can now be repackaged sold and delivered to people in a variety of different formats.

And it is those other formats which will

a) attract people to your website, and

b) start them off on the first few rungs of your value ladder.

Let's be honest about this – to get someone to visit your website (something they will do even though they may have been referred to you by a friend who is one of your existing clients) and then to immediately be expected to commit to your highest value service is a tough ask.

Like anyone looking to make a large 'purchase', they have to be warmed up through the building of relationships and trust.

The content you create and put onto the Internet using your attributes and unique characteristics above is the first step to building trust – and it happens before they even visit your website.

Column 2: Your ideas

You can see from column 2 that your ideas for content can be communicated in several different ways. We've listed just a few:

- Articles/Blogs
- Video
- Live Video
- Podcast
- Webinar
- Micro-Blog (e.g. Twitter, Passle etc.)
- Photos and images
- Infographics
- PR
- Radio and TV
- Slide Decks
- Mobile apps

Each has a part to play in any Content Marketing strategy, and you should choose those which are most appropriate to the people you are trying to attract and serve.

Column 3: Where you post your content

There are a wealth of different platforms which you can use to post your content. Each has millions of users, so the potential reach is huge. But most Financial Advisers are not looking for millions of leads – not even hundreds.

Truth be known, most IFAs are looking for a very small number of very high-quality enquiries – usually fewer than a half dozen per month. But very often these few 'hot' enquiries will still emanate from deep within Social Networking sites.

So a good tactic is to actually ask your existing clients what networking sites they use. Literally ask them at the fact-finding stage if they use Facebook, LinkedIn, and YouTube etc. From this you'll get a good idea of where your clients and future clients hang out online, and then focus your efforts there.

When you do this simple exercise, many Financial Advisers are quite relieved that they don't have to concentrate too much on *all* of the Social Networking sites and can then put their efforts into just one or two. But you must do your homework in the first place.

Post your content – that's your blogs, articles, videos, webinars etc. on these sites – with the express intention of driving readers/viewers/listeners to your website.

Too many Financial Advisers lose heart with Social Media because it doesn't result directly in new business, when their strategy should ideally be to use their expertise to drive traffic to their website **via** Social Media sites, building trust along the way.

An added benefit of putting your expertise-based content on Social Networking platforms is that some of it will hang around to be picked up by Google – again helping to make you visible in search results when people are looking for professionals with your expertise.

This is important because not everyone uses Social Media yet, but they do use search and we want them to find you on the likes of Google and Bing. Having said that, please bear in mind that since 2010 there have been more daily visits to Social Networking sites than to search engines – so Social Media is increasingly important in the search process.

Let's have another look at our strategy overview.

Still in column 3, you'll also see that in addition to adding your content to Social Networking sites, you should also be making sure that your existing clients get to see it too – as well as your professional connections. One tip is to point existing clients to this content via your regular newsletter or to write to them personally highlighting where they can find your content.

This starts to make Social Media something that becomes integral to your client proposition – not just an add-on.

Content creation and marketing is not just to find new clients but also <u>to add value to existing clients</u> and to enhance relationships with local accountants and solicitors. It particularly serves to remind those groups why they have a relationship with you and will encourage them to refer additional people to you.

Column 4: Arriving at your website

The moment someone arrives at your website is critical, in fact it's a make or break moment.

Now it's very possible that someone who leaves without looking at another page may well come back again another time – particularly if they continue to be exposed to your awesome content on Social Networking sites and elsewhere. But we don't really want to run the risk that they won't come back, so we need to do everything we can to:

a) Keep them on our site for as long as possible
b) Make them feel that your site was created for people just like them
c) Engage with them at a human level
d) Build trust immediately
e) Give us their email address

It goes without saying that your website should look good and in this day and age that's easier than ever before. More important than anything else though is that it MUST look good on a mobile device – in fact Google will penalise your site in search rankings if it's not mobile compatible.

Use this tool to check your site:

https://search.google.com/test/mobile-friendly

A good tactic to keep people on your site **and** to engage with them at the same time is to include an introductory video which highlights your people, your location and areas of expertise. Perhaps include some client testimonials in the video and clips of your seminar or other client events. Remember, people buy people – this is critical. It's important in how you use Social Media, it's important on your website and it's important if and when they eventually meet you face to face.

It also needs to be remembered that different people visiting your site are looking for different things. Some will just want to get an overview of your business – an 'instinctive feel' for whether or not you would be a good fit for them, whilst others will want in-depth content on different areas of personal finance. Make sure you cater for both types of people.

If you're not sure what to include on your website, look at others across the profession, but better still - ask your clients once a year in your annual survey. It sounds an obvious thing to do, but actually ask your clients what they would like to see on your site – perhaps from a range of suggestions.

There are many different ways to approach the type of website you create but that's not the purpose of this guide, except for one key thing - your 'Value Point'.

Column 5: Your Value Point

In any other industry we'd call this a 'lead magnet', but whenever I've mentioned this to groups of IFAs or Financial Planners they tend to cringe at the phrase – so we'll play nice and call it a Value Point. But actually, that's exactly what it is – a point where you offer a great deal of value – for free.

Your Value Point should be high up on your home page right where it can't be missed. It's a piece of value that you offer a site visitor for free in exchange for their name and email address. Sometimes you see the Value Point offer appear as a pop-up when you go to leave the site.

In fact, it's a piece of content which they would find difficult to resist wanting to own – and all they have to do is give you their email address in exchange.

For the avoidance of doubt, this is **not** a Value Point or Lead Magnet:

```
COMPANY > NEWSLETTER SIGN-UP

Please fill the form below to subscribe to our newsletter!

Join Our Mailing List

Email: [_____]  [Go]
```

These on the other hand, are Lead Magnets/Value Points:

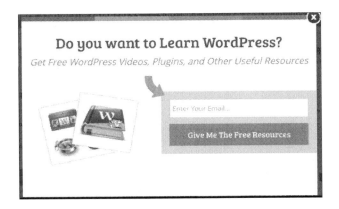

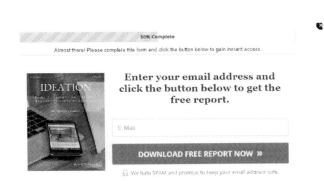

I should stress that these are simply examples and for those of you thinking *"This approach won't work in our market"* I would urge you to think a little more strategically because the world is changing and consumers no longer want just 'brochure websites'. They want, you guessed it – value.

In short, if you want to turn more of your website visitors into clients, you need to find a very attractive way to offer people high value – and the examples above will point you in the right direction in terms of look, feel, concept and design.

What's more they are proven to work.

Yes, the examples above might feel a bit "salesy" as one financial adviser told me, but the fact is that a good lead magnet will often convert about 30% of your website visitors.

You can see that in each example above, they are targeting a specific audience with an offer to match. And in each case, you get real value in exchange for your email address. Clearly you will want to adjust the look and feel of the text/offer for your own market.

What's the potential for a typical IFA/financial advice firm?

So right now, I'm looking at the website statistics for an IFA firm in London which has five other offices around the UK.

They are getting 950 website visitors per month (that's a little higher than average for most smallish IFA firms in the UK), and although we know all sorts of good stuff about how many pages their visitors looked at, how long they stayed on the site, how they found the site, what device they used etc. etc.; what we don't know are their names and contact details. And if we did, that would prove very useful indeed.

At this stage there is little likelihood that they will make an enquiry about financial planning or anything else for that matter. And other than those website statistics, we know very little about them or even why they visited your website in the first place. So the IFA firm needs to find a way to engage with these site visitors – ideally in a way that will quickly build trust.

So if this firm was to create a high-quality value point/lead magnet, they could potentially add around 250 names per month to their list. That's 3,000 per year. Wow.

That's 3,000 people who take the first step onto your value ladder – up which we will encourage them to climb with other expertise and value-based products – some of which they will pay for. This clearly now changes the definition of the word 'client' – something you might want to ponder.

So not only are you converting website visitors into prospects, you are also adding names to your list and creating an additional revenue stream. Some of these people will go right up your ladder over time and will eventually pay for your highest value offering. Many will also refer other people to you along the way.

It is important to remember something I mentioned earlier – the world is changing and more and more visitors to your site will just be looking for information and not a full financial planning service; not just yet anyway. When someone steps on your value ladder you are looking to build trust, such that they don't see financial planning as the be-all and end-all of what advisers offer.

You as a professional Financial Adviser have built up considerable expertise and knowledge over the years and are perfectly capable of creating 'information products' which people will pay for.

But they are much more likely to pay for it if you have given them something of value for free at the earliest stage of the relationship. In short, you are only limited by your imagination as to the kind of products and services that you could sell to your website visitors.

Creating your Value Point offer

Your goal is to come up with an initial lead magnet which is something that makes them excited about owning –

largely because it is highly relevant to them. Only you know what that is likely to be because you know the sort of person who is already a client. You know their typical life stage and you know the financial issues that are probably a priority for them right now.

A good test of whether your piece of value is relevant, is to come up with something that you know they would seriously value and which you could charge money for – but won't.

You've seen the sort of thing – it could be a white paper, special report, eBook, audio course, educational content, webinar, seminar video, assessment or test etc. Something which reveals your expertise and which teaches them something they need to know.

Whatever you come up with, check it against this list:

- It must add a lot of value – and be perceived to add value

- The fact that it is free should surprise and excite them

- It will have taken some work and effort to create – there are no shortcuts to creating something of real value

- It must be a genuine deal – recipients should not feel that they've been hoodwinked or 'short changed' into giving you their email address. They should feel genuinely comfortable about giving you their name and email address

- It is unique to you and your financial advice firm

- It will enhance their perception of you and your firm – and will start the process of building trust in you and your expertise

When promoting your offer on your website, again – work hard on this to make it look enticing. You can either use the services of a graphic designer or use tools such as ClickFunnels or Infusionsoft to help you.

Structuring your offer

You don't have much space so make the most of it. Start with a hook – highlight an issue that is likely to be important to them. It might be a problem that they are probably facing at their particular life stage.

- Be extremely clear in what they'll get when they subscribe

- Be extremely clear about who the offer is aimed at

- Highlight three to five key issues that you address in the offer

- Give a clear call to action – be explicit about what they need to do to get it and when/how they'll receive it

- Keep the sign-up form as short as possible

- Promise you won't spam them or sell their details.

Remember, this offer is not intended to be all things to all people – it is only targeted at people who are likely to be attracted to working with you and your firm.

Many IFAs tell me that they have to work with the 'right' sort of clients, so make sure that your offer has real focus. Quality is key, even at this very early stage.

Column 5: Moving up your value ladder

Remember, the point of doing all this is to build a relationship based on trust through expertise and value. By gaining access to your free product/offer they get to experience your expertise without paying for your highest value service. By building this marketing relationship you are dramatically improving the likelihood of someone becoming a valued client and advocate for your business.

And at the very least you are not wasting/losing website visitors.

Along the route to your highest value service, they will be happy to purchase other information products and services from you because trust is building all the time.

But it's important that I'm honest with you and manage your expectations. Many people on your value ladder will never reach your highest value service – but they are still clients nevertheless.

They are a new type of client for the new world of financial advice.

They are a client that you may never meet, but they are a client all the same. And if you have looked after them with value, they will look after you in a variety of ways from paying you hard cash with their credit card, through to becoming an advocate for your services through referrals and recommendations.

Summary

Social Media is no quick fix for Financial Advisers, but it is an extremely important tool to highlight your expertise, professionalism and credibility, and through which you can send people to your website (or other destination of your choice).

Not every person who visits your website will become a 'client' in the traditional sense of the word – nor would you want them all to be. But they can become a 'client' in the **new** sense of the word, and some of them – the ones you *really* want – will indeed go on to become members of your elite client list.

Finally, you'll remember the financial advice firm in London to which I referred earlier...

Just this week we reviewed the impact that Social Media has had on visits to their website. We discovered that their figures for 2016 compared to 2015 showed:

- Visits via Facebook: UP 435%
- Visits via Twitter: UP 276%
- Visits via LinkedIn: UP 307%
- Visits from search engines: UP between 121% and 279% depending on the search phrase used

Why did this happen?

Because the IFA firm concerned put their focus on posting content of value on Social Media **with the express intention of sending readers on to their website**.

I hope you have found this useful. As I mentioned, it is an overview of a typical value based Social Media strategy for Financial Advisers, but it gives you sufficient detail to get you started on something that will work for your business.

But I promise you that unless you do create your own Social Media strategy – *one that is bespoke to <u>your</u> business*, any business that you do get from Social Media will be by accident at best and quite rare.

So we've tried to make it as easy as possible for you – what follows is a tool that you can use to help build your own plan – it's our **Social Media Strategy Planner for Financial Advisers**.

Simply work through the questions about your business and it will point you in detail to the content that you need to work on that will be most relevant to your target clients.

Part 2:

Social Media Strategy Planner

Introduction to the Strategy Planner

Thank you for your interest in this Social Media Strategy Planner – it is very much appreciated, and we hope that you'll find it valuable and enjoyable to work through.

This planner takes you through a series of questions which are designed to get you thinking more strategically about your use of Social Media and to align it with your business goals and client proposition.

It is relevant to both advisory firms and individuals. Either way, you may find it useful to work through this process as a team or with colleagues to ensure you're all in agreement.

One of the main reasons why many Financial Advisers have not yet fully embraced Social Media is their perception that it's all about marketing – and that inevitably raises questions about compliance. It can be about marketing, but for the most part it need not be. Depending on your chosen platform, your use of Social Media or Social Networking tools can take you down very different routes.

But if your business strategy includes Social Media as part of your overall communication activities, this document will form a valuable part of your plans.

However, this planner will also help you to identify a wide variety of different ways to utilise Social Media to enhance your business and support your business goals.

This planner takes you through several questions about your use of Social Media and the internet. There is no need to over-think the answers, but they are intended to prompt discussion about how effectively (or otherwise) you are using Social Media at a strategic level.

Questions

Please complete as many questions as possible and in detail. The more information you include, the easier it will be to create a Social Media and Content Marketing plan to support your goals and client proposition.

Throughout this activity, we focus on two key areas:

1. Your business goals
2. Your client proposition

There may of course be overlap in some areas, but when answering the questions, try to distinguish between the two because each may require different Social Media tools and activities.

Focus

The purpose of this questionnaire is to help you look at your business in a different way, which in turn will help you to become more strategic in how you use Social Media.

Your answers to the questions will help you to:

1. Identify how Social Media can support various activities in your business

2. Identify target personas to help you connect and engage better with clients and interested parties

through Social Media

3. Identify specific content which you can post on Social Media to support your goals

4. Identify specific Social Media tools you can use to deliver your content to interested parties

Content

At various points this questionnaire refers to 'content', which may or may not be used for 'content marketing'.

What is Content Marketing?

The Content Marketing Institute defines it as follows:

"Content marketing is the marketing and business process for creating and distributing relevant and valuable content to attract, acquire and engage a clearly defined and understood target audience – with the objective of driving profitable customer action."

For financial advisers, this presupposes that 'marketing' is a key purpose behind communicating relevant materials to your target audience, yet that need not necessarily be the case. For example, content in the form of a blog, could be used to simply add value to existing clients, though by its very nature it could also attract new enquiries.

When a financial advice firm analyses its approach to Social Media from a strategic perspective, **the regular communication of high value and relevant materials** should in fact become a core part of their client proposition – from which 'marketing' may become a happy outcome.

In short, whilst financial advice or financial planning is your core business activity, **communicating valuable content should also be viewed as a core activity**.

And at its most basic level, if Social Media users (e.g. prospects) see an inactive Social Media account, they see an inactive company.

Note: When we run Social Media Strategy workshops with financial advisers, most attendees are often surprised at just how many other ways there are for them to use Social Media in their businesses, which go way beyond just marketing.

Online toolkit

Your online content toolkit is only limited by our imaginations, but could include any of the following:

- Blogs
- Articles
- White Papers
- Special Reports

- Case studies
- eNewsletters
- Webinars
- Videos
- Audio and Podcasts
- Website content
- Infographics
- Photos
- PowerPoint and other presentations
- Testimonials (note: not allowed in some countries)
- Skills endorsements
- Tweets
- PR and news
- Status updates
- Online Groups (e.g. Linked, Facebook etc.)
- Corporate updates (Facebook Pages, LinkedIn Company Pages etc.)
- And more.

Let's get started

We're now going to go through a series of statements and questions covering the following areas:

1. Social Media strategy fundamentals – the process
2. Your business and its goals
3. Your clients
4. Your website
5. Your (current) use of Social Media
6. Supporting your business goals with Social Media
7. Supporting your client proposition with Social Media
8. Creating an audience persona
9. Developing your Social Media strategy
10. Important points to note

Let's look at each in turn.

1. Social Media Strategy Fundamentals – the process

Whilst Social Media can be used in a financial advice business without a formal strategy, any 'success' is more likely to be by accident rather than design. And that's OK!

But if you believe that Social Media has even the smallest part to play in how your business promotes itself, engages with others online and attracts new clients, following a process that will lead to a strategy dramatically increases the likelihood of seeing a positive return on your investment.

Typically, the process will look something like this:

- Assess your business: SWOT
- Identify your business goals
- Ask - how can Social/Digital help to achieve these goals?
- Identify client persona
- Identify and/or create content
- Identify tools and actions
- Reach out with appropriate content to support goals
- Engage (and convert if appropriate)
- Measure against identified business goals
- Adjust
- Measure again

2. Describe your Financial Advice business

Write your answers below. Don't forget to SAVE your work if using the PDF version of this planner.

What is the name of your business?

When and how did it get started and how did you first become involved?

What does it look like today?

What changes have you made to get it where it is today?

What are you most proud about the business?

Write an outline/overview describing what your business will look like in two- and five-years' time:

In two years:

In five years:

Now being more explicit - what specific goals do you have for your business over two and five years?

In two years:

1.

2.

3.

If you have more you want to add, write it here:

In five years:

1.

2.

3.

If you have more you want to add, write it here:

What changes/what will you be working on to support these goals?

Looking back in five years' time, what would you regret not having done or achieved in your business?

Why is that important?

What could you be doing better in your business right now?

Why is that important?

What are your 'Business Keywords'? (e.g. Financial Planning, Investment etc.). Imagine if someone typed these words into Google or LinkedIn – what would be the keywords that lead them to you and your business?

List up to a dozen keywords and then rank them in order of importance, so the most important keywords are at the top of the list.

If you can't come up with a dozen, don't worry – list what you can. Also, if you focus on a very tight niche, again it will be unlikely that you can come up with twelve.

1.

2.

3.

4.

5.

6.

7.

8.

9.

10.

11.

12.

Note: These words will form the basis of much of the content which you post on Social Media – particularly LinkedIn if that site is important in your strategy.

3. Your clients

Describe three 'typical' clients of your business:

1.

2.

3.

Are these your perfect, 'dream' clients?

If not, why do you think that is and why have they not been attracted to your business?

Regardless of whether they are dream or ideal clients, how did most of your them become clients in the first place? Write down up to five ways they became clients:

1.

2.

3.

4.

5.

If I met your clients at a party, how would they describe to me what your business does?

If they had written a 'perfect' testimonial for your business and services, what would it say? Write it here:

If you asked them to highlight just one area of your business for improvement or enhancing, what do you think they would say?

Have you ever asked them this question?

Describe below what your perfect, 'dream' client looks like

What do you currently do in your marketing to attract such clients?

List up to five activities

1.

2.

3.

4.

5.

Thinking ahead two to five years (longer if you wish), how might your 'typical' client differ from those you have now?

How or why will they be different from those you have now?

Describe your current referral strategy

Is your current referral strategy written down into your business or marketing plan?

Recommended resource: *Get More Referrals Now!* By Bill Cates http://amzn.to/2e6JqvG

How will new clients discover you and your business in five years' time?

How prepared are you for any changes in how new clients will discover you and your business in five years' time?

Finally, what did you learn from your answers in this section?

4. Your website

You will need to access your website statistics (Google analytics or similar) for most of the questions in the following section. If you don't have access to them right now, take an educated guess at the answers and then compare with the actual figures later.

What are you currently doing to attract people to your website?

How many people visited your website last month?

Is that up or down on the previous month?

Is that up or down on the same period last year?

Last month, what was the split between new visitors and returning visitors to your site?

How many pages did each visitor visit on average?

Which are the most popular pages of your website – and why do you think that is?

Which is the page on your website where most people leave – and why do you think that is?

Now that you know the page on your site where most people leave, what are you going to do about it?

What is the 'bounce rate' on your website? (The percentage of visitors who leave without visiting any other pages)

_____%

How long do visitors stay on your site on average?

What are the top three sources of visits to your site?

Which Social Networking sites drive the most visits to your site?

What search terms are driving people to visit your site?

What time of day do most people visit your site?

Which day of the week attracts most visits to your site?

On which devices are people viewing your site?

When you ask them, how do your clients describe your website?

What do your clients like most about your website?

What do your clients dislike about your website?

What other features would your clients like included on your website?

Have you ever asked them?

What have the answers to these questions told you about your website and your approach to it?

Note: There are a number of analytic tools which can give you this information. In addition to Google Analytics, we recommend a tool called Clicky, which gives you all the essentials but presented in a clear, easy-to-understand format: http://bit.ly/2dFymmH

What typically are your clients' favourite websites?

1.

2.

3.

Have you ever asked them?

What could you learn and what business benefits are there by knowing a client's favourite websites?

What typically are your clients' favourite Social Media sites/tools or messaging apps?

1.

2.

3.

Have you ever asked them?

What could you learn and what business benefits are there by knowing a client's favourite Social Media sites/tools or messaging apps and how could you use this information?

What devices do your clients use to access the Internet and your website?

Have you ever asked them?

What have you learnt by completing this section?

Write down three action points for you or your business that emerge from your answers in this section:

1.

2.

3.

Any other action points?

5. Your use of Social Media as a Financial Advice firm

It has been shown that financial advice businesses that are successful with Social Media have the following characteristics in common:

1. They want to be better at what they do as a financial advice business

2. They know why they are using Social Media (and have a clear plan) i.e. they use Social Media to support initiatives to build a better business

3. They use Social Media a lot – because it is also a part of their proposition

List up to ten different ways that you currently use Social Media in your business. Don't worry if you are only using it a little - just summarise how you are using it at the moment:

Example 1: I use Twitter to contact Providers
Example 2: I use LinkedIn to search for local professional connections
Etc.

1.

2.

3.

4.

5.

6.

7.

8.

9.

10.

What specific results have you had from any of these activities?

What was it about Social Media that helped you to achieve these results?

Social Media is often regarded as purely a Sales and Marketing activity, which naturally will cause many Financial Advisers to exhibit caution.

Contrary to popular belief, advisers *may* use Social Media for financial promotions provided they adhere to normal compliance processes (if in doubt, seek advice from your compliance officer). However, Social Media is far from being the perfect medium for most promotional activity – particularly financial promotions, so it is better to simply not do it.

What's more, consumers have no desire to see financial promotions within their Social Media feeds!

However, Social Media is very powerful when used to support wider strategic business issues, so when considering how you might use Social Media in your financial advice business, you may wish to include one or more of the following outcomes to support the business goals you identified earlier.

Possible outcomes from your use of Social Media as a Financial Advice firm:

1. Attract more visits to website
2. Longer visits to website

3. More pages viewed on website
4. Improve bounce rate
5. Generate more referrals
6. Improve search rankings
7. Help people to get to know us better
8. Give our business a human face beyond traditional face to face relationships
9. Build Community around our clients
10. Reinforce perception as authoritative, expert and credible
11. Build perception of trustworthiness
12. Attract more referrals from professional connections
13. Identify, learn from and engage with niche markets
14. Raise profile in the local community
15. Discover local events where we can raise our profile
16. Be first to spot opportunities to engage with individuals and companies that need our expertise
17. A place where press and media come for help and comment
18. Provide additional ways to engage with clients beyond meetings, newsletters and reviews
19. Provide a way to cement recently new relationships
20. Attract more people to our events by expanding the reach of our promotions
21. Educate people on personal finance, life planning and financial planning
22. Promote new services

23. Decrease our marketing costs
24. Attract people to join our newsletter
25. To sell special digital products (eBooks, online courses etc.)
26. Add another level of 'Wow' to our customer service proposition – further enrich our client experience
27. Promote specific initiatives which go beyond our normal financial advice service – education, local sponsorship, books and articles, public speaking etc.
28. Humanise a topic which disenfranchises some people
29. Build 'buzz' around our business
30. Improve our brand equity
31. Find buyers for our business
32. Find opportunities to acquire other advice businesses
33. Engage with Providers and Suppliers
34. Learn from Thought Leaders
35. Find opportunities to network with other business professionals
36. Attract Internet-savvy new employees
37. Improve staff motivation and engagement
38. Simply give clients another way to talk to us
39. Gain greater insights into the things clients care about – beyond what they've revealed in a fact find meeting
40. Observe our competitors
41. Help us to look active, busy and vibrant
42. Reinforce the tone of voice of our business

43. Highlight testimonials
44. Find, listen to and learn about potential nice markets in which we have expertise
45. People who have been referred to us by an existing client have another way to check us out
46. Learn best practice from other advisers around the world
47. Share best practice with other advisers
48. Mentor younger advisers/new entrants
49. Attract more clients
50. Enhance and develop client loyally
51. Add expertise-based content to your overall proposition

Are there any more outcomes that you would add to this list?

1. **Your business goals**

Having read the list of possible outcomes above, which ones do you instinctively feel could help you to achieve the business goals you identified earlier?

a)

b)

c)

d)

e)

f)

Write any additional thoughts or observations here:

2. Your client proposition

Having read the list of possible outcomes above, which ones do you instinctively feel could help you to support your client proposition?

a)

b)

c)

d)

e)

f)

Write any additional thoughts or observations here:

6. Supporting your business goals with Social Media

6.1 Supporting your business goals with Social Media - Tools

Now that you have identified certain outcomes from using Social Media which could support achievement of your business goals, what are the Social Media **tools** that you should use?

Write down **all** that you feel could apply:

1.

2.

3.

4.

5.

6.

7.

8.

9.

10.

Any others?

From your list, which Social Media tools instinctively feel to be the core/most appropriate for you to use? Let's call these your Core Channels:

1.

2.

3.

4.

5.

Why did you choose these as your Core Channels?

6.2 Supporting your business goals with Social Media - Activities

Social Media activities

Write down three Social Media Channel activities to support your goals and show the purpose and success metrics of each. You can add more activities for each goal if you wish, but our advice is to keep it simple initially.

Here's an example:

Your Key goal #1: Attract more clients and/or referrals

Channel 1: Facebook
Channel purpose: Increase visibility online and drive traffic to website
Channel success metrics: Likes, questions asked, friend requests, 25% increase in site visits

Channel 2: Instagram
Channel purpose: Show pictures of our team; give a human face to our service
Channel success metrics: Increased number of followers on our Instagram account, new enquiries, know staff by names

Channel 3: Blog separate to website
Channel purpose: Enhance perception of our expertise in investments
Channel success metrics: Website visits etc.

Your turn (model the examples above to your own business)

Your Key goal #1:

Channel 1:

Channel purpose:

Channel success metrics:

Channel 2:

Channel purpose:

Channel success metrics:

Channel 3:

Channel purpose:

Channel success metrics:

Your Key goal #2:

Channel 1:

Channel purpose:

Channel success metrics:

Channel 2:

Channel purpose:

Channel success metrics:

Channel 3:

Channel purpose:

Channel success metrics:

Your Key goal #3:

Channel 1:

Channel purpose:

Channel success metrics:

Channel 2:

Channel purpose:

Channel success metrics:

Channel 3:

Channel purpose:

Channel success metrics:

7. Supporting your client proposition with Social Media

Write down three client-facing initiatives that are currently or will soon be a priority in your business:

1.

2.

3.

What do you want to achieve with these initiatives?

Given the list of outcomes and tools available, list between three and ten Social Media activities which could support these client initiatives:

1.

2.

3.

4.

5.

6.

7.

8.

9.

10.

How will you measure success in supporting these initiatives?

We're making progress

By now, you should have a clear idea of:

- Your business goals
- Social Media tools and activities to support them
- Your client proposition and forthcoming initiatives
- Social Media tools and activities to support them
- How you are currently using your website and Social Media

We now need to identify the type of **content** which would appeal to your target audience and encourage them to engage with it via Social Media. To do this we need to create an 'audience persona'.

8. Create an Audience Persona

Think of all types of individual, company or organisations who are important targets for your firm. E.g. Prospects, Existing clients, Professional referrers. Anyone else such as your perfect, dream clients?

List these targets here:

1.

2.

3.

4.

5.

Any others? Write them here:

Now let's look at them in more detail and complete a persona for each.

For 'position' below, this could be anything such as middle management employee, company director nearing retirement, recently retired executive or even retired existing client etc.

Targets and personas can include your existing clients because a key goal might be to encourage existing clients to make more referrals.

Persona name #1:

Their 'position':

Their responsibilities:

Their industry sector or life stage:

Their business type or family situation:

Persona name #2:

Their 'position':

Their responsibilities:

Their industry sector or life stage:

Their business type or family situation:

Persona name #3:

Their 'position':

Their responsibilities:

Their industry sector or life stage:

Their business type or family situation:

Persona name #4:

Their 'position':

Their responsibilities:

Their industry sector or life stage:

Their business type or family situation:

What practical needs does this person have and expect your firm to meet?

Persona #1

Persona #2

Persona #3

Persona #4

What perceived strengths do your firm have for this person?

Persona #1

Persona #2

Persona #3

Persona #4

What are the hot issues in this person's professional and/or personal world?

Persona #1

Persona #2

Persona #3

Persona #4

What emotional needs does this person have and expect your firm to meet?

Persona #1

Persona #2

Persona #3

Persona #4

What are the barriers preventing this person from engaging with your firm?

Persona #1

Persona #2

Persona #3

Persona #4

What are the key messages this person needs to hear?

Persona #1

Persona #2

Persona #3

Persona #4

What life or professional events might trigger interest in your services?

Persona #1

Persona #2

Persona #3

Persona #4

What events within a target company or organisation might trigger interest in your services?

Persona #1

Persona #2

Persona #3

Persona #4

How do these triggers signal themselves and where/how could you hear about them?

Persona #1

Persona #2

Persona #3

Persona #4

Are there any ways that you could use Social Media to hear about these events?

What type of content does this person like to consume and values most? (Have you ever asked them?)

Hint: Here are some types of content which will appeal to different people.

- Facts
- Emotional
- Controversial
- Stories
- Stories about other clients
- Nostalgia
- News
- Inspiration
- Audio
- Video
- Articles/Blogs
- Short form content such as Tweets

- Humour

Persona #1

Persona #2

Persona #3

Persona #4

How frequently do they like to receive content which interests them? (Have you ever asked them?)

Persona #1

Persona #2

Persona #3

Persona #4

Where does this person 'hang out' physically and/or digitally?

Persona #1

Persona #2

Persona #3

Persona #4

What content is this person getting from your 'competitors'?

(Competitors can be anyone or any organisation who creates, curates or distributes content that is relevant to them – not just other financial advice firms)

Persona #1

Persona #2

Persona #3

Persona #4

Where is your Sweet Spot – the area where you have immense authority and expertise, and are uniquely or strongly positioned to talk about? This is where you get maximum response for your effort.

Persona #1

Persona #2

Persona #3

Persona #4

Getting there!

Let's start to pull this together with some key questions:

What insights and ideas are these answers giving you in respect of each persona?

Persona #1

Persona #2

Persona #3

Persona #4

What content could we create in response to your audience's needs?

Persona #1

Persona #2

Persona #3

Persona #4

What is our Tone of Voice and house style in our online communications and content?

I.e. does it reflect our character when clients meet us? Fun, quirky and entertaining, serious and academic or something else?

What are the different ways we could communicate our Tone of Voice through our content on Social Media?

Where specifically will we publish and promote this content? Here are some ideas – choose those which fit your goals and client proposition and prioritise them in a list below:

- Facebook personal page
- Facebook Page

- Facebook Group
- LinkedIn personal page
- LinkedIn company page
- LinkedIn showcase page
- LinkedIn articles
- Twitter
- YouTube
- Podcast
- Pinterest
- Infographic
- Instagram
- Flickr
- Google+
- SlideShare
- Website
- Blog on website
- Blog elsewhere
    - Tumblr, Blogger, WordPress
- eNewsletter
- eBook
- White Paper
- Webinar
- Wikipedia

1.

2.

3.

4.

5.

Add more if necessary:

9. Developing your Social Media strategy

Well done – you've covered a lot of ground and now we need to start pulling it all together. Here's what we know about you and your business so far:

1. Where your business started, where it is today and its goals for the future

2. What typical clients look like, what they think about your business, how they use Social Media and how you might acquire new clients in the future

3. How well your website is working for you

4. How you currently use Social Media

5. How you could use Social Media to support your business goals and client proposition through specific tools and activities

6. How you will measure the success of these activities

7. Understanding your client personas in order to create and fine tune relevant content that will appeal to each

Now take some time to review the answers you have given in each section and draw conclusions as to what specific steps you need to take.

You've already written down most of the answers, but simplify everything with either of these two models below, adapting it to suit your own circumstances.

Strategy Model 1 - Example

Key business or client proposition goal #1

To raise the profile of Jones & Co Financial Planning in and around Reading

Who specifically do we want to appeal to?

Local business owners who are looking to sell or retire within the next five years

Where can we reach them online?

LinkedIn, supporters of local Chambers of Commerce on Facebook and some on Twitter.

What content are they interested in?

Golf and sports, lifestyle and arts, travel, business news.

How do they like to receive and consume such content when online?

Video, audio and blogs.

Content we will create which will appeal to them and regularity

Weekly podcast plus transcription in blog form. The podcast will be themed 'The Reading Business Show'. Call to action to visit website and blog.

Supporting activities

Highlighting on Reading/Berkshire-themed Facebook groups plus Twitter with dedicated #hashtag. Also Reading UK Business Community group on LinkedIn and our Company page on LinkedIn.

Local PR plus dedicated page on our website. Possible alliance with local radio station?

Local sponsorship at Golf and Country Club.

Attend local networking events.

How we will measure success

Increased visits to relevant page on our website over three, six and twelve months.

Greater recognition locally through word of mouth, referrals and surveys and at Chamber of Commerce.

Responses to calls to action.

Repeat this model for up to three key business goals.

Remember – this is your Online/Social Media strategy, but you will have seen from the example that it should dovetail with your offline activities. Each supports the other.

Your turn

Key business or client proposition goal #1

Who specifically do we want to appeal to?

Where can we reach them online?

What content are they interested in?

How do they like to receive and consume such content when online?

Content we will create which will appeal to them and regularity

Supporting activities

How we will measure success

Key business or client proposition goal #2

Who specifically do we want to appeal to?

Where can we reach them online?

What content are they interested in?

How do they like to receive and consume such content when online?

Content we will create which will appeal to them and regularity

Supporting activities

How we will measure success

Key business or client proposition goal #3

Who specifically do we want to appeal to?

Where can we reach them online?

What content are they interested in?

How do they like to receive and consume such content when online?

Content we will create which will appeal to them and regularity

Supporting activities

How we will measure success

As an alternative, try this second model

Strategy Model 2

What are your key business goals?

Who do you need to target?

What interests, concerns and needs of theirs can you address?

What type of content will get their attention?

Where will they see it?

How often do they want to see it?

What tools will you deliver it with?

How will you measure success?

10. Important points to consider

The purpose of this plan is to highlight the importance of aligning your Social Media activities with your business goals and your client proposition.

You have identified key goals and online activities which will support them, and it's important that you monitor progress and adjust tactics accordingly. Of course, your business goals may change or evolve too, so revisit this document as appropriate.

This guide is not intended to be an exhaustive source of Social Media knowledge – the very nature of the Internet is that communication technology and its potential in business is constantly changing. The important point is that you think strategically about your use of Social Media – regardless of whatever shiny new app or Social Media tool comes along next.

In the meantime, here are some important points to consider as you develop your plans.

Write an Editorial Calendar

By creating an editorial calendar, you can help to better organise the curation, creation and frequency of your Social Media posts.

It will also help to clarify when and where your content will be posted. There are many free such calendars on the

Internet, so search around until you find one which works best with your strategy. You'll probably end up designing your own; in the meantime search 'Editorial calendar for Social Media' and adapt it to suit your strategy.

Getting your team involved

It's very important that your Social Media posts reflect the character and tone of the company and the people who spend time with clients – hence the 'tone' questions earlier.

That said, you may want to assign some of your Social Media activities to colleagues so that they become your brand advocates.

It goes without saying that some people will be better at it than others, so here is a list of traits that you should look for when choosing who to let loose with your Social Media accounts:

- Good communicators
- They 'get' the objectives of your brand
- Can articulate the objective
- They evangelise your brand
- Strong sense of Mission/Vision
- Consistent in behaviours
- Factually accurate in communications
- Can handle pressure
- Can handle argumentative people

- Relaxed and friendly – but get things done
- They 'get' and use Social Media themselves
- They are open, random and supportive online
- They can articulate the dangers of Social Media
- They can tell stories
- They are trustworthy
- At ease with all levels of Management – internally and externally
- They know your marketplace and target clients
- Keen to give feedback on own performance
- Fizzing with ideas and quick witted

Who in your firm exhibits some of these qualities?

1.

2.

3.

4.

5.

Train your colleagues

Training is essential if your whole team is to buy into the benefits of including Social Media in your business strategy.

There are still many people who are not entirely comfortable using Social Media, but it's important that they can see its value in the workplace. Training will help, even if they are not keen to get involved themselves or become your brand advocates.

More content ideas - Video

If your persona analysis earlier identified that some targets enjoy and relate well to video content, here are some ideas for how you can use the medium:

- Intro video to add to your LinkedIn profile
- Meet the team
- Interviews with individual members of your team
- A Day in the Life of ABC Financial Planning
- Client testimonials on video
- Seminar clips
- Seminar testimonials
- Client event video
- Promotional 'advert' for your business (add to website and Social profiles etc.)
- Tutorial/How to
- Client case study
- FAQ or commonly asked questions from clients
- You, public speaking
- Expert interview
- Video Blog (Vlog)
- Your take on industry news

- Company news
- Paper reviews
- Weekly Video Update
- Service process walk through
- Pitch or Intro video to local companies
- Walkthrough of tools you use e.g. cashflow modelling
- Educational videos (you could create potentially hundreds of short videos in this area)
- Video email

What ideas of your own come out of these suggestions? Write down five that you feel could work in your business:

1.

2.

3.

4.

5.

Note: Approximately 85% of videos on Facebook are watched without sound turned up. So include subtitles on some of your videos.

Always be learning

Ensure that someone in your business is responsible for staying on top of what's happening in Social Media. It's a fast-changing world, but at its heart, Social Media is all about helping and facilitating communication.

Whatever new tool or site comes along, it will almost always be something that helps humans to interact in some shape or form. Google News is a good source of information.

Another option is to appoint a non-executive digital director – someone to meet with once a quarter (or more regularly) and who keeps you up to date on new technology developments. They should also occasionally challenge you on plans that you may or may not be making.

Recycle existing content to create new content

When considering what content you will communicate to target clients, it is possible that you already have content such as articles and blogs which can be recycled and repurposed. Look out those old articles that you've written and bring them up to date.

Think Themes rather than Topics in your content

Themed content represents a whole bigger picture area you can potentially 'own'.

Themes could be based around things such as:

- Later life planning
- Investing
- Life events
- Protection
- Etc.

Themes can then be broken down into smaller pieces of content:

- Blogs
- Email series
- Infographics
- Presentations
- Video
- Webinars
- Checklists
- Guests posts
- Tweets

- Audio
- etc.

Identify your Theme keywords and ensure that they are used in your online content. In some areas this will help with SEO (search engine optimisation).

Personalisation

Personalisation of content is critical – particularly when engaging with existing clients, and that also includes using people's names in Tweets, on Facebook and LinkedIn.

Remember that sweet spot we mentioned earlier when you create content – the more personalised it is for your target audience, the better response you are likely to get.

Email footers

Be proud of your Social Media activity and ensure that you include links to relevant profiles in your email signatures – and indeed *everything* that leaves your office (business cards, notepaper etc.).

As we highlighted earlier, whilst Social Media supports your business goals and client proposition, it can also be part of your proposition – in which case make sure that your activity is as visible as possible.

Out of Office

We're staggered how few financial advisers include links to their website and Social Media profiles in their 'Out of Office' emails.

We often see things like "I'm on holiday". Yes, literally as short as that! From today, offer people a link to your site and profiles in your email – do it now!

Value of your content

Be conscious of the potential value of everything you post. Whilst the whole point of this guide is to help you to think strategically about Social Media, serendipity also has its place – particularly when you have a large network of contacts.

You can also increase the potential value of everything you post by aiming for the sweet spot we highlighted earlier. When you hit the sweet spot with well-considered content you improve the likelihood of your tweet or post being commented on and shared – and when people share your content to their own network, the potential value of it increases significantly.

Some recipients of your content will inevitably want to share it with their own network of contacts on Social Media, and different people have different motivations for doing so. Here are some of them:

- "Network value" – the impulse to add value to others' lives through valuable and entertaining content

- As a way to support causes or issues that they care about

- Build relationships - to help them connect with others who share their interests

- Self-fulfilment – to feel good about themselves and to feel more involved with the world

- Define yourself to others - to give people a better sense of who they are and what they care about, particularly if it supports our own views.

The source of this information is *The Psychology of Sharing study. New York Times Customer Insight Group.* Again, it is useful to understand this and take into account when creating content that you create and post. Hence it is really important to understand personas as discussed earlier.

Adam Mosseri, VP, Product Management at Facebook puts it more simply: *"It's important to publish content that people want to talk about."*

What spreads content wider still?

- Emotions
- Positive sentiment
- Awe - Amazement, Shock
- Anger - Annoyance, Displeasure, Shock, Indignation
- Anxiety - Worry, Nervousness, Unease
- Sadness - Unhappiness, Grief

Source: What Makes Online Content Viral? Jonah Berger, Joseph G. Campbell. University of Pennsylvania

Ask for action

Persuade prospects and site visitors to take the next step. Everything we have talked about has been about using Social Media to help achieve your business or client goals, but always keep in mind the need to create calls to action.

Don't be afraid to use phrases such as the following in some of your content:

- Take a look here
- You should click here
- Watch now
- Read our latest blog here
- Reserve your place now
- Subscribe now
- Yes, I want a copy

- Start your journey to…
- Join our members
- Get your free…

Influencers, partners and advocates – look after them

We could write a whole book about so-called influencers and their role in enhancing your visibility within their network and niche communities.

In its simplest form, what you want is for an influencer to highlight you, your work and your expertise in their own blogs and content.

This is taking your strategy work to another level, and whilst hard work, can be very profitable. To find out more, search Google for 'Blog outreach techniques'.

The same goes for partners, professional introducers and advocates – spend time working on ways to keep you and your business front of mind, so that they almost feel obliged to highlight you, your expertise and your business in their own Social Media activities.

You may also wish to consider ways to incentivise, thank and reward followers and advocates.

Hygiene factor - Get your profiles right

Having put a lot of effort into planning how you will use Social Media strategically, it's vital that your basic Social Media profiles look good.

There is little point in driving people to your Social profiles if there is nothing for them to look at when they arrive. Make absolutely sure that your profile is completely filled out, has a friendly and professional photo, is keyword rich (see business keywords earlier), highlights your areas of expertise and also includes some personal interests.

It goes without saying that this is particularly important on LinkedIn, but is equally important to get across salient points on sites such as Twitter and Facebook.

Ask for testimonials for your Social Media content

As we mentioned earlier, it is perfectly reasonable and advisable for the communication of high quality content to become a key part of your business proposition, so there is no reason why your Social Media activity shouldn't receive plaudits in its own right.

Just as you would ask your clients for testimonials for the work you do with them, periodically ask them for recognition of your content and the value you provide online. The more targeted your content, the more likely you will receive plaudits for it.

Create style guidelines

We talked earlier about your company 'tone of voice' on Social Media. This could vary from humorous and casual at one end, through to particularly professional and academic at the other. Either way, write down and share with colleagues exactly what your house style is when posting online.

Suggest examples of your preferred writing style and ensure consistency across all Social Networking tools that you use. Clearly, your online style should be appropriate for the market you are communicating with.

Paid Social Media

This guide has deliberately been written to ensure that you focus on matching your Social Media activity with your business goals and client proposition.

In short, using paid Social Media can give considerably greater reach to your content, and this could be particularly useful if 'extending your reach and visibility' is a key goal. But without a clear Social Media strategy in the first place, paid promotions are unlikely to make your content any more relevant to your target audience.

Our advice is to get your strategy right first, apply it for six months to a year and then to consider highly targeted promotional posts. (Contact us for further information.)

Automation

Having established your strategy and are clear about when, where and how often you will be posting content, you may find that you can automate some of your activity.

There is a lot of evidence to show that financial advice firms that are particularly successful with Social Media (and remember that 'success' will vary in definition between one financial advice firm and another) use it a lot. Whilst careful targeting of your content is essential, regular posts at different times of day increase your chances of better supporting your business goals.

There are many tools that you can use to automate your content, but for most financial advice firms, tools such as TweetDeck, Hootsuite and Buffer will suffice – the latter being highly recommended.

Apps

In the UK at least, the number of financial advice firms with their own smartphone app is negligible. It's as though this apparently insignificant piece of software on our mobile device has passed the industry by. Having said that, it's estimated that ten to fifteen percent of financial advice firms still don't have a website, so it was inevitable that developing a smartphone app would not be high up their agenda.

There is a perception that this is a costly exercise but depending on the functionality you want included it need not be. There are numerous 'DIY' tools online to help you create your own app for Android and iOS devices which are very inexpensive – what's more you don't need any special skills. If you can't do it, your kids will help you.

At the very least, learn how to add a link to your smartphone's home screen, which when clicked takes people to your website. Assuming your website is optimised for mobile devices; this will do fine and will give people your full website experience via a button on their smartphone home screen.

Given that most people with smartphones use them multiple times a day, it is logical that they should be able to see your logo on it. We work with one IFA firm and have created a short video for clients on how to add this link to their phones.

Measure everything

How do you know if your Social Media content is reaching your desired audience? Measure it! There are a variety of tools that you can use which need no technical skill:

- Bit.ly

- Twitter analytics
- Facebook analytics
- Google analytics

Bit.ly is particularly useful because you can see exactly how many engagements there were on each and every post that you put out.

After a while you get a sense for what types of content are working well and what isn't. This is vital information and someone in your firm should be made responsible for monitoring your stats and reporting back to you.

In particular, note what happens versus your objectives. Also note:

- Why did it work?
- Why did it fail?
- Share with team

Outsourcing

I'm often asked if Social Media can be outsourced. Of course, it can, but if your activity and content strategy is centred on you and individuals in your firms at a human level (people buy people) - it's important that the content is authentic, particularly when posting on Twitter and Facebook.

For example, if you are targeting business owners who enjoy (say) golf or tennis in your area, whoever you have outsourced the work to must sound genuinely authentic if they are posting about those sports.

There is of course no reason why outsourcing the curation of content shouldn't be done – in fact you can save you a lot of time if you find someone who really understands your objectives and what you are looking for in terms of content that you want to share.

In short, if outsourcing your Social Media activity, as the strategy owner it's essential that you stay extremely close to the project. My advice is that for most financial advice firms, posted content should be highly authentic which means individual advisers and their team being closely involved.

Time

The single most common question that I'm asked by financial advisers is *"How do I find the time for all this?"*

As we've seen, you can get help – either from within your own business or by outsourcing some aspects of your activity. But that question is always asked before the person asking it has thought about the importance of strategy when using Social Media.

If you take the 'give it a go' approach, it will always be time consuming and expensive. But when you take the approach that the communication of high quality and relevant content is actually part of your client proposition, you then realise that time is the least of your concerns.

Social Media is not some add-on that you 'give a go' in your business. In today's marketplace, Social Media is part of what you do and how you add value to clients, and you'll always find time for that.

In actual fact, you've just completed one of the most time-consuming aspects of successful Social Media – sitting down, asking yourself tough questions and making a plan. Once you have a plan, time no longer becomes an issue.

Summary

I sincerely hope you've found this planner and guide useful. It will have helped you to look at your business in a different way and I also hope you found the process valuable and fun.

Whilst Social Media has established itself as a powerful communication tool, I hope you will have seen that it's not necessarily all about marketing. Much of the content that you post will indirectly act as marketing material, but there is so much more that you can do with it. Revisit the Social Media Outcomes section earlier for a reminder.

However you use it, for Social Media to add value to your business and your clients you will need to have a plan.

This planner will have helped you to generate ideas and to create that plan. Now all you need to do is execute it...

What are your next steps?

1.

2.

3.

4.

5.

Good luck!

If you have any specific questions relating to your business – please do get in touch. You can write to me directly at philip@philipcalvert.com

I can also work with you in your business and offer:

- In-house workshops – full and half days
- In-house consultancy
- LinkedIn training
- LinkedIn profile reviews
- Seminar Marketing training
- Skype consultancy
- Monthly mentoring programme
- Conference speaking
- Ad-hoc help by email

Please also join our Facebook group where you can find more resources and network with other financial advice professionals:

https://www.facebook.com/groups/AdviserLifeTalk

Bulk copies of this planner

If you would like ten or more copies of this planner, please contact us for information about bulk discounts.

And if you have found this planner to be useful, please help us to spread the word to others by considering leaving a five-star review on Amazon. Thank you.

Additional Resources for Financial Advisers by Philip Calvert

Successful Seminar Selling for Financial Advisers: The Financial Planner's Guide to Attracting Profitable New Leads through Seminars, Workshops & Client Events.

Get yours at https://amzn.to/2JzMH6Z

LinkedIn Success for Financial Advisers: Tips, Tricks and Connection Scripts Every Financial Planner Needs to Know

Get yours at https://amzn.to/2NpPX5X

56 New Income Streams for Financial Advisers: How to Turn your Financial Planning Expertise & Experience into Profitable Information Products for the Digital Age

Get yours at https://amzn.to/2pZbSJj

About the Author

Philip Calvert - Delivering Actionable Ideas to Make a Positive Impact at your Conference, Corporate Event or Sales Meeting.

Philip is an international speaker and author specialising in helping financial advice businesses to market and present themselves with credibility and professionalism through seminars, live events, public speaking, LinkedIn and wider social media.

A world leading authority on LinkedIn and Seminar Selling, Philip speaks worldwide and delivers high value and entertaining keynotes and breakout sessions.

For further information connect with him on LinkedIn at www.linkedin.com/in/saleskeynotespeaker or send an email to philip@philipcalvert.com.

Visit his website at www.philipcalvert.com

Disclaimer and Terms of Use

This book is provided for research and educational purposes. You do not have resell or giveaway rights for any portion of this publication. Only customers that have purchased this publication are authorised to view it. No part of this publication may be transmitted or reproduced in any way without the prior written permission of the author. Violations of this copyright will be enforced in law.

The information services and resources provided in this book are based upon the current internet marketing and economic environment. The techniques presented have been extraordinarily lucrative and rewarding to information marketers and business owners worldwide, however because the internet is constantly changing, some sites and services presented in this book may change, cease or expand with time.

We hope that the skills and knowledge acquired from this book will provide you with the ability to adapt to inevitable internet and marketing evolution. However, we cannot be held responsible for changes that may affect the applicability or effectiveness of these techniques.

Any earnings, income statements or other results quoted, are based on our own and the testing of other marketers and are estimates of what we believe you could earn. There is no assurance you will do as well as stated in any examples and could be influenced by a variety of factors, not least of which include work ethic and market conditions. If you rely upon any figures provided, you must accept the entire risk of not doing as well as the information provided.

All product names, logos and artwork mentioned in this book are copyrights of their respective owners. None of the owners have sponsored or endorsed this publication.

While all attempts have been made to verify information provided, the author assumes no responsibility for errors, omissions or contrary interpretation on the subject matter herein. Any perceived slights of people or organisations are unintentional. The purchaser or reader of this publication assumes responsibility for the use of these materials and information.

No guarantees of income are made. The author reserves the right to make changes and assumes no responsibility or liability whatsoever on behalf of any purchaser or reader of these materials.

From time to time, the author has included hyperlinks to external products and services, some of which may be an affiliate link, where the author would receive a commission should the reader make a purchase.

The purchaser and reader assume full responsibility for compliance and compliant use of the material in this book, as defined by their respective regulatory body. No guarantees are made by the author that any of the ideas presented in this book will be acceptable under the purchaser or reader's local compliance regime.

Additional Notes

Copyright Philip Calvert 2019. All Rights Reserved.

Printed in Poland
by Amazon Fulfillment
Poland Sp. z o.o., Wrocław